THREE SISTERS

RashDash

THREE SISTERS
after Chekhov

OBERON BOOKS
LONDON

WWW.OBERONBOOKS.COM

First published in 2018 by Oberon Books Ltd
521 Caledonian Road, London N7 9RH
Tel: +44 (0) 20 7607 3637 / Fax: +44 (0) 20 7607 3629
e-mail: info@oberonbooks.com
www.oberonbooks.com

A catalogue record for this book is available from the British Library.

PB ISBN: 9781786824776
E ISBN: 9781786824783

Cover image: The Other Richard

eBook conversion by Lapiz Digital Services, India.

Visit www.oberonbooks.com to read more about all our books and to buy them. You will also find features, author interviews and news of any author events, and you can sign up for e-newsletters so that you're always first to hear about our new releases.

'We should show life neither as it is nor as it ought to be,
but as we see it in our dreams.'
Anton Chekhov

Text by Abbi Greenland with Helen Goalen and Becky Wilkie

Lyrics by Abbi Greenland, Helen Goalen and Becky Wilkie

This was a very collaborative process and all the people in the room made this show.

The people in the room / original production
Olga Helen Goalen
Masha Abbi Greenland
Irena Becky Wilkie
Violin & Synth Yoon-Ji Kim
Drums Chloe Rianna

Dramaturg Jude Christian
Design Rosie Elnile
Lighting Design Ziggy Jacobs
Stage Management Simon Perkins
Sound Engineer Eleanor Theodorou
Zine Design Elisa Nader
Producer Amy Letman

Photographs The Other Richard
Artwork Rosie Elnile

We have experimented with a few ways to document the more physical/visual side of our work. In this script we have opted for descriptions of actions + photographs.

Three Sisters by RashDash was first performed at the Royal Exchange Theatre, Manchester on 3rd May 2018.

A RashDash and Royal Exchange Theatre co-production. Commissioned by Tobacco Factory Theatres, The Yard Theatre, Cambridge Junction, MAYK and Bristol Old Vic.

Supported using public funding from the National Lottery through Arts Council England.

A drawing room. A comfy armchair, an uncomfortable, wooden chair, a chaise longue. A heavy, iron bath. A chandelier almost touching the ground. A drum kit, a piano, a synth, a violin, five microphone stands. A gauze changing room. A ticker-tape sign sits on top of the piano. A toy dog.

Behind the drawing room, from ceiling to floor, a pair of curtains have been drawn shut.

The room is full of colour. Pink floor, orange changing room, green armchair, pink piano stool.

Costume changes are very important in this show. Seeing the costumes and seeing the changes. The changes should take the time they take. The costumes should be selected for maximum fun and pleasure for both the wearer and the watcher.

ART ROOM 1

Costumes: big, fluffy ballgowns. The skirts are big and silly. They take lots of space and rustle when they move.

Black. The sound of a crowd applauding.

Lights.

A white bust of Chekhov is in the middle of the room.

Black. The sound of a crowd applauding.

Lights. A drawing room. Five women sit completely still. They gaze listlessly at the furniture or into the distance. The Chekhov bust sits on a plinth at the side of the room.

Black. The sound of a crowd applauding.

Lights.

A woman is dancing with a lampshade on her head.

A woman is posing with a toy dog.

A woman is swinging the chandelier.

A woman is playing 'Sonata in G', badly.

A woman is standing on a chair and vigorously conducting an imagined orchestra.

Black. The sound of a crowd applauding.

Lights. A drawing room. Scene 1 from The Play. OLGA sits in the comfy armchair, IRENA on the uncomfortable, wooden chair and MASHA is on the chaise, reading a dictionary.

OLGA Father died a year ago today. May the 5th, your birthday Irena. Yes, on this day last year it was so cold it was snowing and I was so sad I didn't know how to go on. You fainted Irena, do you remember? You were lying so still it looked as if you had died, too. But now a whole year has passed and we're talking about it so easily. You're wearing such a lovely dress and you look so beautiful.

Cymbal strikes twelve.

The clock struck twelve then, too. As the coffin was taken into the cemetery there was a military band and a salute with rifle fire; because Father was in command of the brigade. There weren't many people at the funeral though. Maybe because it was snowing so hard.

IRENA I don't know if I want to think about all that today

OLGA Yes, father was made a brigadier and had to leave Moscow and so we all came with him of course. *(A woman starts banging the drums.)* Everything was so beautiful in Moscow – the blossom was

MASHA starts banging her head into the book she is reading.

IRENA switches rhythmically between Happy Face and Sad Face.

The synth player becomes a giant metronome swinging from side to side.

The drummer is banging louder.

The blossom was

*She is banging louder and a synth has come in now too –
bash, bash, bash.*

The blossom was

Black. The sound of a crowd applauding.

Lights.

*Three men in 1901 Russian military uniforms are standing on
the furniture. A man reads from a copy of The Play.*

MAN If a man starts talking about the fundamental or
serious issues of life you call that philosophy, or possibly
just sophistry. But if a woman, or a few women start
philosophising, you call that...well I don't know, what
would you call that? What does it mean when a group
of women talk to each other?

*Everyone thinks about what it means when women talk to
each other.*

Black. The sound of a crowd applauding.

Lights.

Everyone is still thinking. No one has moved.

Black. The sound of a crowd applauding.

Lights.

ARTISTIC DIRECTOR If you want to be taken seriously and
to work on bigger stages and with more resource then
at some point it would be sensible to engage with the
classics. How about *Three Sisters*? That's got three women
in it.

Black. The sound of a crowd applauding.

Lights.

*The men have disappeared. All the women are jumping up
and down and swishing their big, fluffy dresses. They are
smiling directly at us.*

Black. The sound of a crowd applauding.

A guitar is strummed.

Lights.

WOMAN Vershinin makes speeches

WOMAN Toozenbach makes speeches

WOMAN Koolyghin makes speeches

WOMAN Andrey makes speeches

WOMAN Chebutykin makes speeches

ONE, TWO, THREE, FOUR

Men Make Speeches

Why do you always say all the lines?

Why do you always say all the lines?
Why do you always write all the plays?
Why do you always decide what's good?
Why do you make me feel so stupid?

Why do you always say all the lines?
Why do you always write all the plays?
Why do you always decide what's good?
Why do you make me feel so stupid?

Fuck you and your excellent words
Fuck you and your excellent words
Fuck you and your excellent words
Fuck you fuck you and your excellence

More weight, more weight, more weight, more weight
More weight, more weight, more weight, more weight
More weight, more weight, more weight, more weight
More weight, more weight, more weight, more weight

Why are we always telling your stories?

Why are we always telling your stories?
Why are we always praying to you?

Why are we always tossing you off?
Why are we always giving you milk?

Why are we always telling your stories?
Why are we always praying to you?
Why are we always tossing you off?
Why are we always giving you milk?

Why motherfuckers why motherfuckers why?
Why motherfuckers why motherfuckers why?
Why motherfuckers why motherfuckers why?
Why motherfuckers why motherfuckers why?

Men make speeches, men make speeches
Men make speeches, men make speeches
Men make speeches, men make speeches
Men make speeches, men make speeches
Men make speeches, men make speeches
Men make speeches, men make speeches
Men make speeches, men make speeches
Men make speeches, men make speeches

Fuck you and your excellent words
Fuck you and your excellent words
Fuck you and your excellent words
Fuck you fuck you and your excellence

> *A drum begins to keep the rhythm of a clock. Tick, tock.*

> *Everyone gestures to the ticker-tape sign on top of the piano: 'Tick, tock, tick, tock, tick, tock, tick tock, tick, tock' begins scrolling along the screen.*

> *Everyone gestures to the Chekhov bust at the side of the room. The plinth is lit and begins to turn. It turns throughout the play.*

> *The three women that will play the three sisters come forward and change out of their big, frothy dresses into smart, modern dresses. It looks like a classy adaptation of a classic. They look at each other. They move their dresses to a pile at the side of the room. This is the beginning of a pile that will grow.*

They dance together. They fall into each other, turn each other, lie on each other, carry each other...

DRAWING ROOM 1: SPRING

OLGA sits on the comfy armchair, IRENA on the uncomfortable, wooden chair and MASHA lies across the chaise.

OLGA Why can't I do anything positive about homelessness? I asked someone when it was snowing if I could call the number for the homeless charity on his behalf but he didn't want me to. He said he had somewhere to stay that night and that he was just begging for food during the day. I feel so bad when I can't help, but giving money is not the right thing to do and I feel sure about that now because my friend who worked for a homeless charity once told me so. I just can't stand seeing it, it makes me feel quite faint. It gets me down.

IRENA I don't know why but I'm so happy today. Just like I'm sailing along in a boat with big, beautiful sails, and above me the endless, blue sky, and in the sky, little birds floating around.

OLGA It's because it's your birthday and we're having a dinner for you this evening.

You're so sad today, Masha

IRENA I hope no one brings me any presents. I detest presents. Especially expensive ones. It's very kind of people to bring them, but I feel I can never be grateful enough when I open them and it makes everyone sad. Then they just sit in a drawer or on a shelf and gather dust until enough time has passed and someone can be bothered to take them to the charity shop.

MASHA You're such silly and horrible people. Forgive me for saying so, but you are.

IRENA How bad-tempered you are, Masha

MASHA Well if I'm bad-tempered don't talk to me, then. Don't touch me.

OLGA Do you know what I long for? Getting out of the city. Getting out, getting out, getting out.

IRENA Oh to be surrounded by sky and trees and water, so much you can simply get lost in it. To be in forests so dense that you can't get any signal and so even if people wanted to contact you, they just couldn't! To look up and feel so small and so light you could fall up into the blue, just by thinking of it.

OLGA When I was in Thailand I could really feel that I was on the surface of a planet. All the colours are brighter and the smells are stronger. It's like someone has turned up all the dials on life. Nothing is dull or in the middle there. It was the best holiday of my life. Oh how I long to get out of the city.

MASHA I'm going home. Oh I can't go home anymore. I'm depressed today, I'm sad, so don't listen to me.

OLGA Lunch is ready, there's a pie.

A pie appears on stage, as if from nowhere.

IRENA Excellent, a pie!

MASHA I want a glass of wine

OLGA If only I could afford to buy us all a house. So many people have proper jobs or inheritance or their parents buy them one, but that will never be true for us. We'll have to save and save and then move somewhere so piggy and small with two chairs and a sofa and a tiny stove that smokes and then spend years and years sanding floors and painting walls. It will be such hard work.

IRENA I like to work! How good it must be to have a project. To sand and paint and build. Good heavens it would be so much better to work than to be the sort of young woman who wakes up at midday, eats her breakfast in bed and then takes two hours dressing…that would be dreadful!

OLGA Would it? I'd love to be rich. You think you're all struggling along together and that none of you can afford to go out for dinner every night, and then BAM. Another friend turns out to have been sitting on hundreds of thousands of pounds whilst complaining about being poor the whole time. It makes me feel so stupid.

MASHA Talk, talk, nothing but talk all day long!… Having to live in this awful city with the rain threatening to fall at any moment, and then on top of it having to listen to all this talk. All of this is so small.

OLGA These are our lives Masha, the only ones we have. Everything may seem dreadful at the moment, but this feeling will pass. Everything ends eventually.

MASHA Oh time, I know time, I've been here before with someone else, I know it's a process, but can't I just get over him now? When I'm not freshly heartbroken I can never understand why there are s o m a n y stories about hearts and breaks. I always think there must be more important things to think about. But everything is different now.

OLGA I understand

MASHA No you don't you've never felt like this and that's why I can't talk to you.

IRENA Time is a healer

MASHA Time is a cunt. He is a slow, slow bastard cunt that promises and promises and makes you wait and wait and then just breaks your heart.

Forgive me, shall I go back to saying nothing?

OLGA Irena, you look so beautiful in that dress. I hope you're looking forward to this evening.

IRENA I hope that not many people come. When I'm alone with somebody I'm all right, I'm just like most people. But in company, I get anxious and shy, and I talk all sorts of nonsense.

OLGA I could cancel the event on Facebook but it's so late in the day that people might not see it and arrive anyway. And then what would happen if the people you really like don't come, and the people you invited just to be polite, do.

MASHA Everything will be better when my period comes.

OLGA No we won't cancel it and you'll be fine. We'll all be fine. Dear sisters, everything is fine.

MASHA falls off the chaise and lands on the floor. OLGA and IRENA help her up.

IRENA puts a microphone in front of her. She falls back onto the chaise. OLGA stands her up again.

IRENA plays the first chord. MASHA falls over again. OLGA helps her up again.

IRENA plays the first chord again.

MASHA sings.

I Won't Go Quietly

I won't go quietly
I won't go quietly
You disappeared so quickly
I hope you're in agony
I want to let you go
But I won't go
quietly

I want you to bite your tongue
on the memory
the memory of me
I want you to catch your hip
on the corner
as you walk around me
I want you to cut to cut to cut
the soft chicken skin
between your fingers
on an old envelope
addressed to me

I want you to get on the 175
And see someone you recognise
And it's not me you realise
She has a bigger nose and fatter thighs

I want you to think you feel me
I want you to think you smell me
I want you to want to party
But never be never be ready

I want you to dream of me
like I dream of you, like I dream of you
pulling gently on my nipples with your teeth
like you used to, like you used to
and waking up with bleeding gums
sitting up too
quickly you bash your head on the thought
what have I done?
What the fuck the fuck the fuck have you done?

OLGA takes off MASHA's dress and changes her into a long, red ballgown as she sings. OLGA also changes into a ballgown – green.

Something tickles your throat
and you pull out
a long red hair
Months after we parted
parts of me are
still there
It gathers beads of saliva
and mucus from your throat
You want me to go quietly
but I won't I won't I won't

I want you to think you feel me
I want you to think you smell me
I want you to want to party
But never be never be ready

I want you to dream of me
like I dream of you, like I dream of you
pulling gently on my nipples with your teeth
like you used to, like you used to
and waking up with bleeding gums
sitting up too
quickly you bash your head on the thought
what have I done?
What the fuck the fuck the fuck have you done?

OLGA changes IRENA into a blue ballgown.

OLGA sits on the comfy armchair, IRENA on the uncomfortable, wooden chair and MASHA on the chaise.

DRAWING ROOM 2: SUMMER

OLGA You look better today, Masha. You look quite pretty. Time is doing its work, that's good. I'm glad to see you look a little brighter. I think tonight's party will cheer you up.

IRENA What time will everyone arrive?

OLGA There'll be lots of men. Not for anything serious, you understand, just for fun. What's the matter?

MASHA Just the same as always. Sorry, I know I'm not a pleasure to be around at the moment.

IRENA I'll have to play the piano all night tonight – a lot of rubbish tunes I suppose… Oh well!

MASHA That clock is so loud. Why has it got so much louder?

OLGA Tomorrow I'm free. Heavens, what a joy! Tomorrow I'm free. What will I do?! I will plan all of the cleaning that I need to do and the shopping and I'll organise that cupboard and change the address that my bank has because that hasn't been right for ages and I'll try and meet up with a friend for coffee but she won't be available at such short notice which will give me an extra hour for sitting on the sofa and staring at my phone.

IRENA I can't hear the clock

MASHA It's so loud it's giving me a headache

IRENA I received a text message today to say that my blood has been used at a hospital in St Petersburg. I hope it saved someone's life. I just want to help people. That's all I want. You know how you long for an ice-cold drink of water in hot weather? Well, that's the way I long to help.

OLGA You've always been such a kind person. Even when you were a child, you didn't understand why everyone was sad all the time, but there you were, playing your piano and making people smile.

IRENA I used to feel so talented and special and then I got old and everyone was expecting a great deal from me. I can never live up to their expectations now.

OLGA When we've got out of the city there'll be space to create and there won't be all this noise all the time.

All this clamouring noise and all these other people trying to be heard above the noise. Then you will be able to write and play and hear yourself think. Then you will open the curtains each morning and be welcomed to the day by the light and the fir trees and maples and birches and the scent from a sea of flowers drifting up through your open window. Yes, that is the environment in which to create. Don't you agree, Masha?

MASHA I keep trying to imagine him with other women in order to persuade myself to move on, but it's not the sex that hurts me. What I yearn for is to lie next to him again and have his legs weaving around mine like seaweed and his heavy arms reaching for me in his sleep. I want to smell the work on him again because he would never take off yesterday's t-shirt before getting into bed and he stank of such a beautiful human smell.

.

I know you're starting to get bored of how sad I am. You tell me it's fine for me to go at my own pace and you know it takes time, but you're bored and I'm bored and there's nothing I can do about it.

OLGA I'm not bored. I'm glad you're talking about it.

MASHA Well I'm not. It's been months now, but yesterday I nearly cried in Morrissons, in the cereal aisle, because I bumped into someone I hadn't seen in ages and she asked me if I was ok. People shouldn't ask unless they're ready for you to cry, unless they actually want to know how you are.

IRENA Well I've just this minute decided that I'm going to help people by creating. Everyone needs art. Everyone needs to see themselves reflected in art. I am going to write music and songs that will help people and Masha, I'll start with you.

MASHA Do you have to?

OLGA There's going to be a quiz! I've taken great care in organising a quiz especially for this party. We'll get into teams of five or so and then I will ask questions in lots of different categories like 'Capital Cities' and 'Famous Dictators'. I've also organised everything for a fruit punch and a variety of different cocktails. I think it's going to be quite jolly. Did you just roll your eyes?

MASHA No, I think it sounds wonderful.

OLGA You think you're too cool for my organised fun and that my quiz is silly. Well it's not. Everyone will enjoy it, you'll see.

IRENA I mustn't have any espresso martinis. If you see me holding one, you must knock it out of my hand immediately! They make me cry. And talk a lot of nonsense.

OLGA I am only going to drink two drinks this evening, because that's the perfect amount for making conversation with people I don't know very well and it is also my limit for not getting a hangover at my age. And I shall drink plenty of water. I shall drink a glass of water and then a glass of delicious wine and then a glass of water and then a cocktail and then another glass of water before bed.

MASHA I'm going to get drunk tonight, whatever happens. I hate parties. They're just full of thirty-year-old women talking about how they got engaged and where they're looking to buy and I can't bear it. I just want to shout at everyone that their conversations are terrifying me and then make them leave. I shall get drunk so I can listen to them all without imploding, and so that all the things that are full of meaning to me now can be forgotten.

OLGA I'm going to get up so early tomorrow. You'll all be groaning in bed with sore heads and I'll be up and eating hot cross buns. I can't wait for the morning! The morning is my favourite time of day! Everything is downhill after that. Let's sing something.

MASHA Urgh!

MASHA and IRENA leave.

OLGA sings.

Fun is a Rebellion

In a room of one's own
I can sit on my throne
Lounge in my dressing gown
Get dressed up and go to town

I can take a hot bath
Close my eyes in the dark
Listen to the radio
I can move real slow

Slow slow slow
This is where is where I want to go
Slow slow slow
This is my kind of flow
Slow slow slow
Getting ready for the show
Slow slow slow
Let's go

Girls just wanna have fun
Drinking with abandon
Not going to waste my time
On a fucking shit wine

Monkey climbing
Blah blah
Swinging from the rafter
No need to quieten down
Sing it sing it loud loud

Slow slow slow
This is where is where I want to go
Slow slow slow
This is my kind of flow

Slow slow slow
Getting ready for the show
Slow slow slow
Let's go

Swimming pool dive low
Crasssh let the water flow
Ice cube crunch it
Ready aim fire and spit

Whiskey in the warm breeze
Drifting into dream sleep
I know where I want to go
Down for my solo

Glitter pop
Bubble gum
Fun is the
Rebellion
You can watch it
If you want
Watch me be a selfish cunt

I'm here to run around
Round and round turn upside down
Only reason I'm here's
To swing from the chandelier

Roooaaaaar
I can be a lion too
Rooooaaaar
Is this not acceptable?
Roooaaaarrrr
You're gonna hear me
Roaaarrrrrr

DRAWING ROOM 3: AUTUMN

IRENA and MASHA are sitting in the drawing room. IRENA, MASHA and the two musicians are dressed as four members of the Spice Girls. They watch as OLGA changes into the fifth and final member.

OLGA sits on the comfy armchair, IRENA on the uncomfortable, wooden chair and MASHA on the chaise.

OLGA is looking at her phone. IRENA is sketching MASHA. MASHA is using a cuticle stick to push her cuticles back.

OLGA I am so tired. I didn't sleep at all last night. I just keep watching the videos of the smoke billowing from the tower, knowing I can do nothing. It's so hard to watch a tragedy unfold and be able to do nothing. I just keep updating my news app and feeling so sick. It makes me feel so faint. It's happening in our city and I can do absolutely nothing.

IRENA I'm going to go on the march. There's a march being organised and we should all go.

OLGA If only there was something we could do.

MASHA That clock is driving me crazy. Does it really not bother either of you?

IRENA I was trying to write a song this morning. I got up early and went for a walk and was feeling so full of inspiration. But then I got home and realised I have absolutely nothing to say. Nothing at all. It's so hard being happy and content all the time.

OLGA I think I might want to have a baby soon, but I'm terrified of how much childbirth is going to hurt. I keep dreaming of a giant head trying to come out of my vagina. I can't bear to think of the ripping.

MASHA That's a pathetic thing to say. You should just massage your perineum with vaseline for two weeks before, I've heard that works very well.

IRENA I came off the pill last week, because I want to have a baby soon, too! That will give me something to do!

MASHA sings at them. No words, just non-verbal wailing.

IRENA What are you doing? What is she doing?

OLGA Masha, you won't get more than two out of five for good conduct

MASHA Why? I'm not doing anything. You're only imagining it. In fact, you're only imagining that we exist whereas in reality, we don't exist at all. We're all just figments of some old, white guy's imagination, saying versions of what he thinks we would say. You don't know anything, no one knows anything.

IRENA Don't worry Masha, you'll find someone soon.

MASHA I don't want to have the conversation again about what I do with my pubic hair, or where he should aim when he comes. I did all that with someone I loved, I can't be bothered to. (*MASHA sings again, the same phrase*).

IRENA stops her – puts her hand over her mouth.

IRENA What about that man from the party? He was so clever and charismatic, he was philosophising his head off all night! You love doing that.

MASHA Maybe I spent too long with the wrong man and I've accidentally left this all too late!

MASHA breaks the clock. The drums clatter as it falls apart. Then.

The drummer starts playing a rhythm. It's attractive. MASHA goes towards it. The drums get more interesting. MASHA starts dancing.

The violinist gets up and starts dancing too.

OLGA Masha, sit. Masha, stop it. Masha, sit down. Shhhhhhhhh.

IRENA FINE!

IRENA gets up and goes to the curtains to start opening them.

OLGA Irena, what are you doing now? Where are you going? You can't just leave.

IRENA I just want to see the view.

OLGA No! We always keep the curtains closed in here.

IRENA I just need to see outside for a moment

IRENA opens the first curtain to reveal – a different view. A lightbox with a collage of famous, classic art with photographs of the company that have made the show mixed in with them...

OLGA What's wrong with everyone?

Masha, stop it now

MASHA points at OLGA and starts singing the phrase again, this time with the words.

MASHA Olga olga olga olga olga olga olga olga

OLGA Irena, not both of them, no. You've had a look and that's enough!

IRENA I just want to let some light in and to see that view

IRENA draws the other curtain to reveal more light, more art, more collage.

IRENA Ah! / **OLGA** No!

MASHA is dancing / worshipping the lightboxes.

IRENA joins her.

OLGA What are you doing? You look mad. I don't know what to do.

MASHA is rubbing herself against the furniture.

OLGA Masha go to your room if you want to do that. You can't do that in here.

That's enough Irena, I'm closing the curtains.

As OLGA tries to get to the curtains, IRENA tries to stop her. The three sisters begin to wrestle. It is awkward at first. They are trying to communicate. They are trying to push each other over. They are trying to pull each other's skirts up so that everyone sees their pants. They are trying to pull each other's pants down.

This is accompanied by a gentle waltz.

After landing in a heap on the floor, MASHA gets up and starts to play the first chords of her next song on the piano. IRENA offers to play instead. MASHA doesn't want that. IRENA insists. OLGA is in the bath.

MASHA sings.

Hold a Room

I think my friends imagine me with a man who can hold a room
Mmmmm
I think my friends imagine me with a man who can hold a room
He can hold the whole room
But I would prefer, I would prefer
I would prefer, I would prefer
A man
Who can hold me

There's a kind of man
A man that has all the moves
A man with a plan
Your families and friends approve

He's natural and free and
Everyone says he's such a wit
It all comes so easy
When two worlds come together and fit

He's full of stories full of facts
He won't let the time elapse
He fills the air with boom and pow
He spreads his legs with room and wow

I think my friends imagine me with a man who can hold a
room
Mmmmm
I think my friends imagine me with a man who can hold a room
He can hold the whole room
But I would prefer, I would prefer
I would prefer, I would prefer
A man
Who can hold me

What if I want a scrub?
A man who sometimes doesn't give a fuck
Who sits in the pub
Drinking and coming unstuck

What if he isn't steady
And doesn't know what he wants from life?
He's lost and not ready
For kids, a house, a job or a wife

The one who hangs at the edges
Never bullshits never judges
He parties hard and racks up debt
He smells like cigarettes and sweat

I think my friends imagine me with a man who can hold a room
Mmmmm
I think my friends imagine me with a man who can hold a room
He can hold the whole room
But I would prefer I would prefer
I would prefer I would prefer
A man
Who can hold me

A drum solo. It sounds like a heartbeat, and then becomes an explosion, and then sounds like a heartbeat again.

Synth begins arpeggios. Dreamlike.

OLGA sits on the back of the bath and sings.

Great Expectations

When I remember there is an ending
That one day we will all be gone
No one will remember us
And we will all be forgotten

The noise becomes quiet and still
A space is cleared inside my mind
I open up, it all pours out
And everything is fine, is fine

Swimming to the edge of responsibility
My body floats in the dead sea
Ignoring the why, when and how
I can be anything, anything now

You won't find me when I go
I'll be gone it won't ever matter
When I was lost, when I didn't get it right
A tiny dot in a tiny life

Knowing I will die
Is when I feel most truly alive
The end is in sight
And all that matters
Moves into the light

Remembering that there's an ending
Makes all the rest disappear
Nothing can terrify me
When the end is near

A place to get away from
Being the wrong thing
From all the time spent looking
For how to be the everything

Knowing I will die

Is when I feel most truly alive
The end is in sight
And all that matters
Moves into the light

Everyone leaves except IRENA.

IRENA *doesn't know what to do. A spotlight is on her. She goes to speak – the spotlight moves to the piano. She follows it. She doesn't know what to play. She finds a book with Tchaikovsky music in it and begins to play. After a short while she starts playing her own things instead. Then she sings.*

It's My Moment

It's my moment
It's my time now
and I don't know what to say
Can we hold it off?
Can we pack it all up come back on another day?

Come on ideas
Come on inspiration
Can I get a muse up in this room?
I'm struggling to choose
My words here
Will someone tell me what to do?

It'll be all right
Trust your fucking instincts
Trust that you can get it right
Stand in the spotlight and bathe in it
You deserve it
It's your space now all you've got to do
Is fill it

Second round now
Ting ting the bell rings
and I still don't know what to say
Can we call it off?
Can we pack it all in, come back another day

Come on insight
Come on strong opinions
The words to right the world
Are in my head
But every time I try to speak
I say what's already been said

It'll be all right
Trust your fucking instincts
Trust that you can get it right
Stand in the spotlight and bathe in it
You deserve it
It's your space now all you've got to do
Is fill it

   Big piano solo.

ART ROOM 2

The rest of the company enter behind the drummer playing a military roll on a snare. They are chanting.

CHEKHOV CHEKHOV CHEKHOV CHEKHOV

They are wearing cheerleading outfits with a big C on the chest. IRENA stands centre stage in the wrong costume. They change her, violently, in silence. They give her pigtails.

Music begins. Pop drums and synth.

A trolley of big, old books is wheeled on.

WOMAN 1 and 2 read the books and are delighted by what's inside.

WOMAN 3 sits down with the Chekhov bust and points and flexes her toes.

WOMAN 3 Good toes! Naughty toes! Good toes! Naughty toes!

WOMAN 1 and 2 put the books on their heads and perform basic ballet steps, whilst keeping the books balanced.

WOMAN 2 piles all the books on top of WOMAN 1. WOMAN 3 stands with the Chekhov bust and watches them. WOMAN 2 stands on top of the books, on top of WOMAN 1 and looks like a classic painting of Jesus.

WOMAN 3 reaches up to her for a moment of

A pop dance routine. Chekhov Cheerleading.

DRAWING ROOM 4: WINTER

The sisters arrive in the drawing room wearing their cheerleading outfits and realise it's not right. They change frantically into three very large bear costumes.

MASHA is looking at her phone. IRENA is reading one of the very big, old books. OLGA is stroking the dog.

MASHA I went on a date last Saturday and he was very lovely and sexy. It was nice to fancy someone again.

OLGA Everyone's moving away. I can't believe they're going. It was such a wonderful time when we all lived so close. We could simply get up and say, I fancy seeing my friends today! And within a moment, we'd be there with avocados and freshly squeezed orange juice and sourdough bread from the fancy bakery. But now it's all slipping through our fingers and everyone's getting out except us.

IRENA I read a great deal, but I never know which books I should choose, and I probably read a lot that's not worth much at all. No matter how much I put in, my brain seems so empty. How little I know! How little!

OLGA I don't understand when you're reading books. How do you have the time? What am I doing that means I don't have the time? Is it that you don't watch *Celebrity Bake Off* or *Gogglebox*? Well more fool you I say. I don't feel guilty about it at all. Masha, what are you doing?

MASHA Swiping

OLGA I'm so glad you're getting out there again. You're a beautiful and clever woman and you put up with more than you should have in that relationship. He would always do whatever he wanted whenever he wanted and was so selfish all the time. He got up so late and made such little effort with your friends.

MASHA I used to think he could try harder, that his aloofness was just another man expecting another woman to do all the emotional work. I thought that by demanding more from my relationship I was standing up for all women, everywhere. But now that he's no longer here, asking for more time and more space, I wonder if he was just a person that needed more time and more space and if the thing hanging between his legs, that I will no longer feel full of desire, between mine, had nothing to do with it.

A military drum roll.

IRENA Listen! That must mean they're leaving. I thought they were going to come and say goodbye. We don't know when we'll see them again. They're going so far away and the trains are so expensive.

OLGA We've said goodbye to everyone already.

MASHA I wonder if feminism has ruined my life

OLGA Don't be ridiculous, you're the biggest feminist I know. You're always talking about it. It just takes one man to leave you and you abandon all your values!

MASHA He's not just a man, he's a person that I loved and that couldn't manage being close to me and my demands. Why did I keep pushing all the time? Why didn't I just let him be who he is? Why did I make our differences about what I do or don't deserve? Because of feminism. Stupid, stupid feminism.

IRENA It's too hot for the time of year and you don't even seem worried about it.

MASHA When you read a novel everything in it seems so old and obvious and you imagine your life will make the same kind of sense. But then you find yourself on Tinder at thirty and you realise you have to take your happiness in snatches.

OLGA I wasted so much time in my twenties being anxious and trying to be good at everything. Now I'm thirty I feel different. More powerful. But I can already feel the time approaching when no one cares what I think anymore.

Over the course of the following lines they change from the bear outfits into –

OLGA: pink, velour tracksuit bottoms, sparkly bra, diamond Tudor headdress

MASHA: sequin hotpants, ruff

IRENA: glittery, chainmail knight hat, flesh-coloured pants

MASHA When will I want to fuck other people?

IRENA When will they arrive to say their goodbyes?

OLGA When will I get to leave this stupid city?

MASHA When will I meet someone I want to make love and a family with?

IRENA When will people stop treating me like a child?

OLGA When will I earn enough money to have a baby?

MASHA When will the rents get so high we have to move outwards again?

IRENA When will I be able to tell a room full of my friends a story without my palms sweating?

OLGA When will I actually delete my Facebook account?

MASHA When will I frame up and become a fucking vegan?

IRENA When will I have something to say?

OLGA When will this play stop being performed?

MASHA When will people stop marking my work out of five?

IRENA When will people stop telling me if my work is good or not?

OLGA When will I be able to do a handstand?

MASHA When will I get up early enough to meditate before work?

IRENA When will this city disappear under water?

OLGA When will something dramatic happen to me that I can make dramatic art about?

MASHA When will I have my children?

IRENA When will people be worried about this weather?

OLGA If only we knew

MASHA If only we knew

IRENA If only we knew

OLGA If only we knew

MASHA If only we knew

IRENA If only we knew

OLGA If only we knew

MASHA If only we knew

IRENA If only we knew

ART ROOM 3

They dance together, landing in the poses from posters for productions of Three Sisters or clichéd images of three women together.

WOMAN 1 breastfeeds Chekhov.

WOMAN 2 dies in the bath, beautifully.

WOMAN 3 rides a dog like a horse.

WOMAN 1 winds Chekhov and then dances with him.

WOMAN 2 dies in the bath, beautifully.

WOMAN 3 finds a spinning top and watches it decelerate, slowly.

WOMAN 1 is dressed as Henry the Eighth. She sits in the armchair and reads from a newspaper, reviews of previous productions of Three Sisters.

WOMAN 2 makes love to and sacrifices herself for the bust of Chekhov.

Reviews song

We can't include the next song for copyright reasons, but new versions of it can be assembled.

This song lasts about fifteen minutes and is made up of extracts from reviews of popular/recent productions of Three Sisters.

For this production all the reviews happen to be by male critics.

The extracts we selected highlight

— the way reviews can sometimes label some artistic choices as 'good' and some as 'bad'

— the way reviews can sometimes label some artistic choices as 'correct' and some as 'incorrect'

— how reviews analyse a director's choices when they 'take on' classics

— how reviews analyse the appearances of women who play characters in the classics

— how reviews measure the current artists up against the classic writer

In our production we replaced all the names of directors and actors with the word 'Woman' or 'Man', as appropriate.

The song is broken into three phases.

Phase 1: The reviews are spoken over music, they are read aloud from a newspaper.
Phase 2: The reviews are spoken rhythmically over music, they are no longer read.
Phase 3: The reviews are rapped over music. The music is loud and pumping.

It ends with the repeated singing/chanting of

*not good not good not good not good
very good very good very good very good
not good not good not good not good
very good very good very good very good
not good not good not good not good
very good very good very good very good
not good not good not good not good
very good very good very good very good*

The violinist plays a KILLER VIOLIN SOLO.

The lights come up around her as she plays.

Everyone changes into traditional 1901 costume. They help each other. It takes time. The lights are up.

DRAWING ROOM 5

Five women sit in the drawing room together. They are looking at us.

Black.

Lights.

The women are hugging.

Black.

Lights.

The women are hiding behind the furniture.

Black.

Lights.

The women are taking up lots of space.

Black.

Lights.

Five women sit in a drawing room together. They are looking at us.

IRENA Something else now

They turn over the furniture to reveal recreations of classic pictures but featuring women in the company that have made the show. A woman clutching tennis balls to her breasts. A woman's arm showing her muscle.

Black.

Lights up.

They all sing.

Work

Work work work
Work is pure
Work work work
Work for more
The future will be beautiful
If we work
It's our fucking duty to
Work work work

Don't work for the money
Work coz it's good
Work for the many
Don't work coz you should

Work for the space
Work for the freedom
Work for the others
Because we need them

Work work work
Work is pure
Work work work
Work for more
The future will be beautiful
If we work
It's our fucking duty to
Work work work

Work for the future
Work for the kids
Work for the birds
Work for the pigs

Rihanna said we got to work work work work work
Britney said work, bitch
Missy said work it
We all say work
So show me how you work work

Work work work
Work is pure
Work work work
Work for more
The future will be beautiful
If we work
It's our fucking duty to
Work work work

Work for the body
Work for the brain
Work for the different
Don't work for the same

Work for the country
Work for the soul
Work for more power
Don't work for control

Work for the unheard
Work for the unseen
Work for the unhappy
And all in between

Just keep working
Because it's begun
Work to continue
The rebellion
The rebellion
The rebellion
The rebellion

End.

WWW.OBERONBOOKS.COM